THE EXCELLENCE EQUATION

THE EXCELLENCE EQUATION

A formula for achieving what you want out of life

ED MONTGOMERY

Ed Montgomery

The Excellence Equation

A formula for achieving what you want out of life

Published by Spines Publishing Platform

ISBN: 979-8-90222-806-6

Spines

Contents

Introduction

I've been in Sales most of my life, and for the majority of that involved managing other salespeople. I've spent a ton of time reading books on Sales, attending seminars, listening to Sales trainers on tapes, and just thinking about what can be done to keep getting better. Afterall, Sales is a very black and white business; you're either getting a check or you're not. Learning how to get more of those checks is important. So, I absorbed years of experience, hours of audio books and presentations, and read reams of literature on the subject.

All of us have heard dozens of people use the phrase "formula for success" or something similar when pitching their take on how to make it rich. They're always saying it's a secret, too, as if the gazillion people publishing books, doing videos, LinkedIn master classes, or Ted Talks were actually trying to hide something. The "secret" was everywhere.

But in all of that, I never saw an actual formula. You know, a mathematical equation that laid it all out for me. The geek in me wanted to see numbers, letters, and math symbols in a clean equation that one could follow in order to succeed.

No secret.

Just something someone could use to plug in different decisions and actions, then have the confidence that they would get a particular result.

I had been watching YouTube videos of Neil deGrasse Tyson and Chuck Nice talking about quantum physics and other scientific subjects that I thought were pretty cool. I already said I am a geek. I admit it. I kept heading down that rabbit hole and learning more about mathematical equations and how the purpose was to simplify complex equations as much as possible, considering variables, constants, etc., and reducing all of this down to its simplest mathematical form. Reducing these expressions to their simplest form is a fundamental skill in math and it makes it easier to explain the core of a problem, which then makes it easier to attack even more complex or advanced topics.

This was exactly what I wanted to do, and I figured I was smart enough to pull it off. I mean, I learned how to solve the marginal propensity to consume in Econ, and I've watched every season of "The Big Bang Theory." With a little effort, I knew I could pull this off. I was going to create a formula that would be inclusive of a lot of information but simple enough to remember and apply.

Then other people, smarter than me, could pick it apart, or apply it to more complex issues and accomplish something really amazing. Me, I'll settle for helping people make decisions that will bring about a fulfilling life, by following a straightforward formula.

I needed to begin this process by identifying the key factors that impacted success before figuring out how to quantify that impact. So, I started writing down all the little phrases and quotes I've learned over the years that were about succeeding at something or avoiding pitfalls. I remember all of these catchy little things because they're simple. And I'm not much of anything other than simple. Plus, I remember funny stories and experiences. Those two traits have served me well over the years, so I lean into them.

But I wanted this to be useful, not like the fact that I can recite the label of a Budweiser beer, so I sought out other sources.

I talked to a few of my very successful friends and colleagues, dove back into the business books I've kept, doodled equations, read LinkedIn articles, listened to podcasts, watched vlogs, and kept watching YouTube videos on sales, success, and math. And here's where I made the switch from a formula to achieve success to one that achieves excellence.

First of all, success can be defined in a lot of ways. Some people have even said that it's not an end or a goal, but it's the path to getting there that makes success. And we've all heard about pursuing perfection—"practice makes perfect!"—and that's what I wanted to get to for this formula and this book. But perfection is a lousy goal because it simply doesn't exist. It's good to have lofty goals but foolish to have impossible ones. Knowing something has zero chance of succeeding, but going after it anyways is a recipe for failure, and that's not what any of us want.

Instead of pursuing perfection, I learned we should pursue excellence. It's still a high bar to clear, and some goals should take a lot to reach. Excellence can only be achieved over a range of time and through a pattern of good results. To achieve it, we don't have to be perfect, but we must be good repeatedly. To do that, we have to continually learn, practice, and execute at the highest level we can. We also need to keep raising that level, which takes more learning, practicing, and execution. When we do that, we can look back and see excellence.

Wayne Gretzky wasn't perfect. He had off nights, missed opportunities, and wasn't the absolute best at every aspect of the game of hockey. But over time, his natural talent, combined with his work ethic and passion, led to a career of excellence. The same can be said of any top athlete, politician, pastor, teacher, or whomever. Excellence is earned over time.

So, here's what I came up with:

$$\mathbf{E=[(P+O)e^3]C}$$

Where:

E = Excellence
P = Preparation
O = Opportunity
e^3 = Enthusiasm, Energy and Effort
C = Consistency

To achieve excellence, one must apply enthusiasm, energy, and effort when preparation meets opportunity; all of this must be done consistently.

Pretty straightforward and succinct. Not necessarily easy, but simple.

I believe this sums up what it takes to succeed: to achieve excellence in business and in life.

You can stop reading right here if you like, but I think it's important to talk more about what this means and how I got here.

Excellence in Business

In the business world, excellence is what goes with you from job to job. How you rise through the ranks, earn more money, handle more responsibility, and gain more stability will depend on your track record.

That last one, "stability," is key in today's business environment.

Job security has become almost mythical, and it makes sense. Businesses are cold, unfeeling entities. It's important to understand that and also to understand that it's not a bad thing. That cold nature, black-and-white mentality is how a business maintains its existence. Revenues have to exceed expenses consistently, or the business dies. Economic forces are dynamic, constantly changing, and that means that businesses are going to face hard times regardless of how great the humans are who are running them.

Keep that in mind as you go through life. Be aware of your company's economic health and what factors impact it. If you do that, you'll hardly ever be surprised by a layoff, and at least you'll be better prepared.

So, when it comes to job security, remember this: your stability lies in your mobility.

Having a track record of excellence makes you mobile. But a track record isn't created in a moment, which is great because it isn't going to be without negatives. You're going to mess up, make mistakes, get beaten by someone better, or just have bad luck. But because your record is built up over time, that means there's always a way to put together some successes. The more often you can do that, the better your record becomes.

Which means you need to keep track of those successes as they happen.

Create a document or spreadsheet that you plan to keep with you forever. It will need to be something mobile or easy to copy and reproduce because technology is going to change, you are going to move, and life is going to throw things at you that will be complete surprises. This document could be in pretty much any format you like, but here are the key things you should write down: start with a description of the win. It doesn't have to be pretty or grammatically correct; it's just for you, but it needs to have the specifics. For instance, if you won a sales contest at work, write it down. Five years from now, that may not be something for your resume or for an application, but it could be in the short term. If you win “Salesperson of the Month,” write that down. Make a note of the company name, your territory, your sales figures, and how many people were on the sales team. The more you compile on this document, the clearer your track record becomes, and that will do great things for you when it's time to get a promotion or a bigger and better job.

After a while you'll be able to start deleting things that are no longer a big deal, but others will begin to pile up for you. Like being the top salesperson in a given month. After several years you might be able to say something like "was top salesperson eleven times at two different companies." Or something like "acquired more new customers than any other sales representative in 2028." Those are the types of things that will matter to a recruiter or sales manager that wants to hire strong talent.

Make sure to be specific as you document your successes. The numbers matter; even if you feel like there needs to be context, trust me, the context will come at some point, and you need to have those numbers ready, and they need to be real. Exaggerating or lying outright will come back to bite you. This document will help you prove what you’re claiming and help prevent you from saying something that isn’t true by accident.

I also moved away from “sales success” as the goal of my formula after speaking with several of my friends. While sales is an important skill for pretty much any businessperson to have, it’s not the primary goal in business.

I'm fortunate to have grown up with several people who achieved some serious levels of success. Fred is now a Distinguished Engineer with IBM; Ron and Mike were CEOs of different companies, Dwayne is still a CEO, Paul is a retired high school principal, and Jack was one of the founders of iGov.com. I've known Fred, Ron, and Jack since the fifth grade! I wanted to know if there was something about us, something in our stories that others could imitate to improve their odds of future success. So, I began by interviewing them. Okay, we basically hung out and talked, but a couple of the conversations were very interview-like.

One of my favorite parts of those get-togethers was reliving stories about things we did that impressed or amazed us. Ron, Jack, Fred, and I were all in the same fifth-grade class together and had some great stories to share.

Ron recalled a time when we had to do an oral book report in front of the class. Fred was called up to do his report; he walked to the front of the class holding a piece of paper and started to read it. Ron said that everything seemed to be going along just fine, but then the teacher interrupted Fred and asked to see his paper. It was blank! Fred hadn't done the assignment but didn't hesitate to get up and act like he had done it. Ron was amazed by the guts Fred had to try to pull that off. Fred told me, “Fake it till you make it,” when I asked him about it. He'd read the book, forgotten about writing his report, and figured he might get away with winging the oral report part.

I remember being similarly impressed by something Ron did. We all had to sing a solo in front of our music class in sixth grade. Of course, we were all terrified by this and knew it was going to be embarrassing, especially if the girls laughed at us. But when the day came, Ron volunteered to go first, got up, and sang with a lot of enthusiasm. He just threw himself into it. Now, he's not a bad singer, but he's not great either. It was his fearless approach that struck me. Ron said he just figured it was easiest to get it out of the way, and no one would remember how good or bad he did.

Jack and Ron told a story about me, too. It was how I handled speaking in front of all the students in the school at an assembly. My sixth-grade teacher was the student government advisor, and he saw something in me beyond my insecurities. I wasn't popular enough by any means to get elected to an office or even picked by someone to be on a committee, but Mr. Prohaska created a new committee and made me the chair. The Poster Committee was supposed to review and approve any posters that were going to be put up around the school, ensuring they looked good, were laid out well, and had no spelling mistakes. I don't know if there was an actual need or not, but he created it anyway and told me I was in charge of it, which meant I had to give a report in front of everyone several times a year.

That first assembly was the one that stuck in the minds of Jack and Ron. You can imagine how a sixth grader might handle walking up to a podium and reading a report they had written carefully with their parents or teachers. Not familiar with a microphone, standing on a little stool so they could be seen over the podium, and shakily delivering what was written down.

I didn't do that.

"You just walked out to the middle of the stage and delivered!" Ron said. "You had all this confidence, and everyone could hear you. I was amazed."

My memory of that is that I knew I had to show the example posters I had made, so the podium wasn't an option, and I was so scared that people wouldn't know what I was saying unless I pretty much yelled, so I did.

In those discussions, it became clear that we all had different strengths and weaknesses, and we achieved our success through different paths. Sales was mixed into a lot of those paths, but only a couple of us had that as our primary business background. What became clear to me was that my formula wasn't going to be about just achieving sales success, but about something more. These guys were all doing something similar that led to careers of excellence.

Between my discussions with them and what I had learned about setting a good goal, "excellence" became the right target.

So, I asked them, "What does it take to achieve excellence? What advice would you give someone to get there?"

The floodgates opened...

PART I

Preparation (P)

1

Prioritize and Plan Ahead

Quick observation on "Luck"

MY GRANDFATHER USED TO SAY, "I'd rather be lucky than good any day." He'd then point out that being good took work, but getting lucky didn't. I've also heard Mark Cuban discuss luck in a documentary I watched about him. In it, he said that if a billionaire ever tells you they didn't get lucky, then they're full of shit.

Here's what I've learned: Luck isn't really a thing. It may not even exist. I think the best explanation about luck is that it's what happens when preparation meets opportunity. We either prepare with intent, or it's just part of our lives when an opportunity appears. In that moment, the fact that we were prepared for it creates what we call "luck."

We are constantly preparing ourselves for some opportunity in the future. The question is whether or not we're preparing ourselves with intent for a particular type of opportunity.

"Begin with the end in mind" - pick a general direction.

It's important to at least have a sense of the direction you want to go before heading out. You don't have to have a specific location or goal in mind, but you need to know the general direction you want to go. This way, when you learn something new, discover a mistake, or run into some sort of resistance, the adjustments you need to make are smaller. You're still getting closer to where you want to go, even if you must change directions or shift something else.

This is easier to do once you've set specific goals with defined tasks that will help you reach your desired result, but it's tougher to do when you're just starting out in professional life and aren't sure at all what you want to be when you grow up.

In the following chapters, I'll share the advice my friends and I felt was important to pass along about thinking ahead.

"Live with Intent"

In high school, I had a fantastic English teacher, Mrs. Jones. She taught us so much more than grammar, syntax, and all the things she'd probably cringe about if she ever reads this book. "Oh, Ed. Where did I go wrong with you?" I can hear her asking with that half-smile she'd give. She also sparked my interest in Shakespeare and how literature can kick our imagination into overdrive, transport us to incredible places, and make us believe that we can make a difference, too. But an exercise she had us do made such an impact on me that I've never forgotten it and still ask myself the same questions of myself today.

She had us get out a piece of paper for a pop quiz. I remember everyone groaning. She told us she was going to ask us a question, and we were to write down one, maybe two-word answers. Make a quick list right off the top of our heads. The question:

How do you want to be remembered when you die?

I'm pretty sure everyone looked up abruptly, and she just waved at us to start writing. I don't remember all of what I listed, but I know there were "funny," "kind," and "cared." Five minutes of silence as everyone just wrote away. Then she told us to turn the paper over to answer the second question.

"What are you doing right now to be remembered that way?"

Silence. A pause.

She then explained that we didn't really have to write anything on the second side of the paper, but we should do more than just come up with answers. We should do those things. Every day. Because that was the only way the front side of that paper would ever come true.

Going through your days with that in mind is living with intent, and living with intent is how you accomplish things.

Take a little time to write out some goals for yourself, starting with how you want to be remembered. Then, add some professional goals—big picture, general things. Putting together the details will come later, but for now, keep it big and way out in your future life.

Then start living each day in a way that can lead you there.

Set Priorities - Decide what's most important.

Learning how to prioritize will help you make decisions that will enable you to live with intent. It's not always easy, but there's a great metaphor out there that really clarifies things: the "rocks in the jar" story.

A professor began a class by putting a big, empty jar on top of a table at the front of the lecture hall. Then he pulled out several large rocks and placed them in the jar until no more fit. He asked the class, "Is the jar full?"

"Yes," a few of the students answered. Then he brought out a bag of pebbles and poured them into the jar until they were at the top. "Is it full now?" he asked. "Yes!" the students answered. But then he brought out a bag of sand and began to pour it into the jar, shaking it now and then until no more could fit. "How about now?" he asked. Some students said, "yes," but a couple said, "no." The professor smiled at the ones who said, "no" and picked up a cup of water. He poured it in.

The professor then explained that the jar was their life. It could be a year, a month, or a day, but it was a limited unit of time. And the rocks were the big things that really mattered, like health, happiness, relationships, and rest. The pebbles, sand, and water represented a sliding scale of all the other things that take up time in our lives. He pointed out that if he had started by putting any of the other things into the jar before the big rocks, then the big things wouldn't fit. They would be left out. Missed.

Know what is important and make sure to do the things you need to do when you need to do them in order for those big things to make it into your jar.

Student Takeaways

- Decide what is most important to you in the long term.
- Take actions in the short term that move you toward your long-term goals.

- It's okay to not know a specific destination, just a general direction.

Reflection Exercise

1. Take Mrs. Jones's quiz.
2. How do you want to be remembered?
3. What can you do today to be remembered that way?

Application Challenge

Each night for the next week, make a list of the things you did that moved you toward your "how I want to be remembered" goal. Then, jot down a couple of things you know you can do the following day to keep moving toward it.

Having a plan and working it –(parents cringe here)

Most of us are raised to believe that the "correct" way to do school is to chase A's like a trained seal chasing fish: class -> study -> test -> grade -> repeat. Nobody ever asks the more important question:

"What's the actual goal here?"

When I got to college, I realized my goals were different. I wanted the full experience: playing sports, meeting new people, going to parties, and saying "yes" to life.

So, I did something most people wouldn't even consider: I got my syllabus every quarter and strategically chose which assignments and tests I was going to skip.

I took zeros. On purpose.

Because I planned for it. I'd look at the calendar to see which tests fell after weekends I knew I'd be busy. If I wasn't going to give a test the time it deserved, I didn't pretend I was. Then I'd do the math to make sure I could still average a passing grade. My GPA was trash, but guess what? I graduated on time. No summer school. No makeup classes. No panic. And I got exactly what I wanted out of my college experience.

You know what they call the people who graduate in the bottom half of their class in medical school?

Doctor.

"C's get degrees, baby."

I'm not telling you to blow off school. I'm telling you this: if you're honest about your goals, you can build a plan that serves you. Most students never pause long enough to ask what they actually want. I did, and it worked—because I planned ahead.

Student Takeaways

- Don't let other people define your success.
- Be intentional—even if your path looks different.
- "You can't do everything. Decide what matters most."
- A mediocre outcome that matches your priorities beats a "perfect" one that isn't yours.

Reflection Exercise

1. List your top three goals in school right now.
2. Which weekly activities support those goals? Which do not?
3. What can you cut, reduce, or restructure this week to focus on what matters?

Application Challenge

For one week, track how you spend your time daily. Then compare it to your goals. If your calendar doesn't reflect what you say matters, your actions are lying for you. Fix it.

Jack & the Soda Rule: Money + Values

Growing up, my buddy Jack would go to McDonald's with us, buy a burger and fries, and always drink water. Not because he was broke, but because soda was a bad trade. He valued the fries more than the fountain Coke.

At the time, we thought he was weird. He didn't care. Later, we learned that sodas are the highest-margin items on the menu. Jack intuitively understood value—and lived by it.

My cousin-in-law plays the same game. He and his wife love wine but never order it at restaurants. They can buy an entire bottle for the cost of one glass. So, they order and eat dinner, go home, and drink great wine together. Over the years, that small choice has saved them thousands—money they spent on what they actually value: cruises.

They traded the short-term ego boost of "I'll have a glass of Cabernet" for long-term experiences they cared about. That's the point: spending is a reflection of values, not income.

Student Takeaways

- Know what matters to you—not what looks "cool."
- Small financial decisions compound over time.
- You can have almost anything you want—just not everything.
- Money is a tool; aim it at what you value.

Reflection Exercise

1. List three things you spend money on each week.
2. Rank them by value (not cost).
3. What could you cut or reduce with almost no loss of happiness?
4. What would you rather save toward? (Travel, laptop, business, car, etc.)

Application Challenge

Track every dollar you spend for seven days. At the week's end, ask, "Do my purchases re!ect what I say I value?" If not, adjust next week's spending to match your values.

Get to a spot to take a shot—position yourself for opportunities.

I went to a seminar on coaching little basketball once, and one of the points the instructor made gave me a real "aha" moment. He talked about teaching the players what to do when they don't have the ball. It was like a chess match because everything each of them did caused the defending team to do something in response, which meant the offense could literally control the defensive players.

His example was how a guard would bring the ball down the center of the court, then move slightly to their right as their defender engaged them. As they moved to the right, they would accelerate slightly. While that was happening, the other players were lined up with two players out to the sides and two in the paint: one toward the top of the key and one under the basket. As the guard made their move to the right, the two players in the paint moved toward center court and to their right. This brought their defenders with them and cleared the lane. Meanwhile, the offensive player on the outside and to the left of the guard with the ball ran to the middle of the court between the top of the key and half court, causing two defensive players to get on top of each other along with the offensive player coming out of the lane toward half court. This made it possible for the outside offensive player to peel off their defender and be all alone behind the guard with the ball who was moving towards the basket.

Because of all this movement, the guard with the ball now has several options that could lead to an easy score. One is to drive all the way to the hoop because they beat their defender, and no other defender has dropped in to help. If a defender does collapse in to help, the guard can easily either pass to their right to a now-open player with a clear shot, or they can pass the ball straight back to the now-open player right behind them.

That's a lot to visualize, I know, but as he was describing this and walking us through it, the message was clear: everyone should get to a spot to get a shot. It may or may not be them getting the shot, but because they moved the way they did, someone was going to be open. Any one of them could end up with the ball, so all of them have to be ready.

The same thing is true in business.

Your actions, your moves, should be working for you or your team towards a win. You start with the goal you have, whether it's making a sale or getting a meeting, and you map your way towards that by doing things that help get you into the best position to achieve your goal. The coaching instructor kept saying, "Get to a spot to take a shot." I've repeated that to myself multiple times in life when a deal was stalled or when what had been working now wasn't.

2

Start Before You're Ready

Jack's First Drum Set - Start Where You Are

MY FRIEND JACK wanted to learn how to play the drums and be in a band, but his parents didn't have the money to buy him an actual drum set. With what Jack could pitch in, they were able to get him a bass drum, a snare drum, and a cymbal. They didn't have enough money for a stand for the cymbal yet—just the cymbal. He also didn't have a stool. Most kids would probably wait to start practicing and keep saving up so they could get the right gear together first.

Well, I came over to Jack's house once and heard him practicing downstairs. There he was, sitting on the couch with the drums in front of him and a cymbal hanging from a string attached to the ceiling, just working on the standard four-count rhythm. Jack wasn't waiting for perfection; he got good enough to play with bands and even made his own because he was starting beats perfectly—every time.

Most people say they'll start when they get the gear, the time, and the confidence. They never start. Jack hacked a kit together and built skill.

A phrase that pays:

> "A journey of a thousand miles begins with a single step."

You may not be able to see the finish line when you start but start just the same. It's only one step. Then it's just another single step. Keep taking them, and you'll get there.

Student Takeaways

- "Do what you can with what you have."
- Skills come from doing—not from gear.
- "Perfection is the enemy of progress, and more is the enemy of enough."

Reflection Exercise

What's something you've been delaying because you lack gear/money/time/confidence? Why are you waiting?

What's the smallest version of starting you could do today? (20 minutes, 200 words, 1 mile, 1 sketch)

Application Challenge

Start it today — messy. 20 minutes of real practice. Do it every day for a week. Watch your skill jump.

"Coaching T-Ball and Soccer: Master the Basics"

Even before I had my own kids, I started coaching sports. You can learn a lot by putting yourself in the position of a teacher. Coaching young kids taught me how to simplify things so they were easier for the kids to learn. Plus, it made it easier for them to move on to more complex aspects, like which base to run to when you get a hit.

In T-ball, I realized that this was going to be the first year in sports for these kids. They were four years old and clearly had a lot to learn about a complicated game. So, I decided to focus on the basics. On our first day of practice, I taught them how to stand. Did you know that when it comes to hitting, fielding, or throwing, you pretty much stand the exact same way before taking action? It's true! Feet apart about shoulder width, knees slightly bent, your hands in front of you just below your chest, facing out about eight or ten inches away from your body, elbows bent. Relaxed but ready.

From that stance, you can step into a throw, move to catch a ball, or swing a bat.

We practiced getting into the ready position, then imitating a throw, imitating a swing, and imitating a catch of a grounder, a toss right at us, and catching a pop-up. All pretend, but all the right movements.

Every one of those kids would pop into that position whenever I yelled, "Ready!" And when the moments came, they could throw, hit, and catch balls. Knowing what to do after those actions took some more time, but they all had confidence in handling those basics.

The first soccer team I coached was five-year-olds. Because I had played the game myself a lot and seen tons of little league games, I decided the thing I wanted them to learn more than anything else was how to stay spread out. If you've ever seen a little kids' soccer game, you've seen them swarm around the ball like a bunch of bees. Not effective at all.

So, in practice, I would get them into their positions and just work on them staying away from each other. They learned lanes and rectangles on the field and how to stay in theirs. I also lined them up close together before going on the field in their positions. This way, they could see who was in front of them to the left and right, who was beside them, and who was behind them. The rule I enforced was that they were never to go ahead of the teammates in front of them and never to go to the other side of the ones beside them. If one started coming close to them, they were supposed to move away.

The result was that when a game started and the other team collapsed around the ball, there was only one of my players in that scrum. The ball would inevitably pop out of the crowd, and my players were the only ones there to trap it. The first one would just kick it downfield, where another one of our teammates was alone, who would kick it again to another wide-open player, who would then score. That team went undefeated, and we never scored fewer than eight goals in a game.

Student Takeaways

- Fundamentals create confidence.
- "Simple beats complicated when you're learning."
- Don't chase advanced tricks before mastering the basics.
- Most failures are skipped "Step 1s."

Reflection Exercise

What skill are you trying to improve right now? List the three fundamentals that underpin it.

How will you practice those fundamentals 10--15 minutes daily this week?

Application Challenge

For 7 days, practice one foundational skill 10-15 minutes/d (footwork, free throws, scales, typing, note-taking, push-ups). Success is built on invisible basics.

3

Context and Conduct

Learning How to Behave – My Dad

BECAUSE MY DAD was an officer in the Air Force, he taught us how to behave like professional officers. We learned how to shake hands and look people in the eyes when we spoke. When we ate dinner, he made sure we knew how a table was set and what different utensils were used for during a meal. He would explain why those things mattered and when they mattered. So, when we did go to a formal dinner on base or with other dignitaries, we looked like we belonged.

He also taught us that there was no job or station beneath us. In fact, by jumping in and helping "dig a ditch" with others, it showed them you were in it with them.

In private, he told risqué or even off-color jokes, but that was just for him and me. Although he never cussed in front of me or my siblings, I had been around other fighter pilots and knew how he had to talk around them. But that was part of what he was teaching me. Certain words were only used in certain places. Different rooms demanded different behavior.

Learn the codes, and you'll move comfortably anywhere.

Student Takeaways

- Context dictates conduct -- read the room.
- Learn the basics: greeting, eye contact, introductions, and table manners.
- Professionalism isn't stiffness; it's respect for context.

Reflection Exercise

Which environments make you feel unsure about how to act?

What two social skills could you practice this month?

Application Challenge

Attend one event outside your comfort zone. Practice eye contact, clear introductions, and one thoughtful question for each person you meet.

Mike's Rule – "Recreational" Means "Recreational"

Growing up, this group of friends and I were pretty hard partiers. It was the late '70s and early '80s, and man, did we enjoy that era. My friend Mike doesn't keep those times a secret from anybody, and he's barely backed off, even as CEO. I asked him how he handles being the fun guy that he is, but also the leader of his company, and he explained it perfectly.

"When it comes to recreational drugs, the operative word is recreational. Show up to work drunk or stoned, and you're fired—right then." He sets those expectations, and others, early and clearly. That way, there's hardly ever a problem.

In life, different places demand different behavior. Clear rules protect opportunities.

Student Takeaways

- Set clear expectations early; confusion creates problems.
- "Your reputation is built on the decisions you make when no one is watching."

Reflection Exercise

What personal rules guide your choices?

Where could clarity help you avoid future problems?

Application Challenge

Write a simple personal conduct code for yourself. Keep it visible for a week and evaluate how it affects your decisions.

PART II

Opportunity (O)

4

Position Yourself for Opportunity

Making Friends Fast: Networking

I MENTIONED that my dad was in the Air Force. As I grew up, we moved a lot—seven times before I turned 12 years old. Every time we moved, my siblings and I had to make new friends. We knew we wouldn't stay in the new place too long, so it was important to find and build new relationships quickly. I remember getting to our new house in Colorado, and while my dad and mom moved the furniture into the house, they told us to go find friends.

My sister was seven, and I was five years old. We started out at the house next door, knocked, and when someone answered, we'd say, "Hi, we're Donya and Trey, and we just moved in there. Donya is seven, and I'm five. Do you have any kids our age?" They either did, or they knew where some were and would point us in that direction. Within a couple of hours, we would have met pretty much every kid in the neighborhood.

This taught me how simple it was to meet new people and strike up conversations. I would learn about them, and they would learn about me—mainly figuring out how we could have fun together, but later in life, it was about how we could work together.

That habit became networking, sales, and opportunities. I think every good thing in my career traces back to that one behavior: I was never afraid to knock on a door—literally or figuratively.

Student Takeaways

- Life rewards people who make the first move.
- Most people are waiting for someone else to speak first—go first.
- Relationships are compound interest on opportunity.
- "You don't need confidence—just curiosity and repetition."

Reflection Exercise

What "interesting but scary" option is on your radar right now?

If the downside is small and the learning is significant, why not take it?

Application Challenge

Apply to one opportunity outside your comfort zone this week (city, country, industry, function). Even if you don't get it, you'll practice taking bigger swings.

5

When Preparation Meets Opportunity

Dwayne & Ray Charles – "Be Ready"

SOME PEOPLE THINK life-changing opportunities are luck. As I've said, they aren't. Luck is where preparation meets opportunity—multiplied by action.

Dwayne had always wanted to be the world's greatest DJ. He loved music, and getting a crowd fired up and dancing made his day. He didn't really know how to make money doing this exactly, and his family didn't have much money at all. So, he was always working at jobs he was able to get while also working for free at radio stations or just playing music on his own or at the high school radio club. His jobs were almost always at bars or restaurants. He would bus tables, clean, and eventually become a cook, DJing at night if the bar had the room, but he worked constantly. His mom pressed him to go to college, though, and he and I went to Virginia Tech together. However, when his grants ran out, he couldn't work enough and stay in school at the same time. So, he worked his butt off for a few months to earn the money to go to school the next semester. Then he would drop out again to work some more.

Around this time, Dwayne was working in a restaurant in Blacksburg and dating a girl who was doing extra work on the filming of the movie "Dirty Dancing" up near Roanoke, VA. Dwayne went to pick her up one day, and the casting folks heard his voice (it's ridiculously low and just cool) and asked him to audition for a part as one of the members of the resort band. The extra money looked really good, so he borrowed a trumpet from a friend and practiced "air trumpet" to prepare for his audition. He planned to take a week off from all three of his jobs to go work on "Dirty Dancing," but he needed to get some things in order first. So, he went into the Chinese restaurant where he was a DJ at night to clean his albums and pack things up. The doors were open; it was a Monday afternoon, and a bunch of guys walked in. It turned out to be Ray Charles's band. He struck up a conversation, hung out with them for a while, and pointed out things they could do in town. His experience as a DJ (seven years of work in radio and clubs), his love of music, and his obvious work ethic combined with organizational skills created a unique opportunity. These guys recognized it, and they happened to have an immediate need. The band asked him if he would be interested in being their stage manager for Ray's upcoming international tour.

Dwayne never showed up for "Dirty Dancing" and spent the next two and a half years traveling the world, working with Ray Charles.

One of my favorite memories of this was the night—I think it was around 3:00 a.m.—that Dwayne called me. He just wanted to tell me he was in the Canary Islands and Ray was on stage performing. That was it. Just my friend letting me know something really cool was happening right then.

Dwayne didn't just "get lucky." He had been preparing for years, so when the moment arrived, he could say, "I'm ready."

Student Takeaways

- Opportunity rarely gives notice—be ready.
- Your preparation is the ticket in.
- Hustle in what you love, even when it doesn't pay off yet.
- "Luck" finds the person who is already doing the work.

Reflection Exercise

What's something you could talk about for 30 minutes without prep?

What's one step you can take this week to deepen that skill: practice, video, blog, club, or mentor?

Application Challenge

Spend 5 hours this week doing — not watching — the thing you want to be great at. Skills compound; opportunity finds the prepared.

Car Sales Meeting – Honest Self-Assessment

I had fallen into the car business and was sitting in a sales meeting where the sales manager was asking each of us about the prior day's activity and what we thought we would close by the end of the month. One of the other sales reps started out by saying he had had several good conversa-tions with people who had come into the dealership when the sales manager interrupted him and told him to stop.

"I don't want to hear about 'good conversations.' Those are BS! Did you close anything, or is anyone coming back today to buy?"

It was pretty harsh and not the way I would handle a moment like that, but it did make me realize that it's easy to look for even little positives in business and convince yourself they're better than what they really are. There's no benefit in pretending there's an opportunity when there really isn't.

Making a sale is black or white; you got a check, or you didn't. Life often works the same way: you either delivered the outcome, or you didn't. Being honest about that isn't negative—it's how you improve.

Keep this in mind, though: it is important to be self-critical, but don't be self-defeating. The idea is to acknowledge failures so you can find ways to move toward success.

Student Takeaways

- Track outcomes, not "vibes."
- Self-assessment must be honest, not self-defeating.
- Define clear metrics before you start; grade against them afterward.
- Progress begins when excuses end.

Reflection Exercise

"What result are you currently 'sugar-coating'?"

What is the clear metric that defines success for it?

What will you do this week to move that metric?

Application Challenge

Pick one goal and define the binary outcome ("done/not done"). Commit to a deadline. Report back to yourself with no spin.

PART III

e3 (Enthusiasm, Energy, Effort)

6

Confidence and Learning

"Go Big: Learn Faster by Being Wrong"

I WAS in a sales training class, and the instructor asked a question. Someone answered, but sort of timidly, you know, where they raise their voice at the end of the sentence because they're not sure, and it sounds like they're asking a question. The instructor told us not to do that anymore in his class. Instead, he wanted us to state our answers firmly and loudly as if we were completely positive about the answer. "Say it like you mean it!"

If we were right, then we'd sound like we were experts and get a little emotional rush from being so authoritative. If we were wrong, we'd be spectacularly wrong, and everyone would laugh. In that case, we would be embarrassed, but hearing the correct answer would be ingrained in our memory, so we'd be able to get it right in the future and avoid that embarrassment.

He let us know that the class was the safest place to "blow it big." We were there to learn, so we should do what would help us learn most effectively.

Student Takeaways

- Confidence accelerates learning.
- "Being wrong out loud beats being silent and stagnant."
- "Embarrassment is temporary; growth is permanent."
- The world rewards people who speak up.

Reflection Exercise

Recall a time you stayed quiet even though you had an idea. Why?

What topic could you practice out loud this week to speed up your learning?

Application Challenge

Raise your hand first once per day for a week. Say your answer confidently. Right or wrong, reflect on what you learned.

Get excited - Enthusiasm sells

I learned a great lesson while in the car business that explained why I had already been successful as a salesperson. Enthusiasm is magical when it comes to helping someone make a positive buying decision. Think about it. How motivated are you to buy anything from someone who seems bored or unhappy to be doing what they're doing? I know I've literally walked out of a shop where the person there was completely uninterested in why they were there.

My sales manager at the Pontiac store where I worked would say, "Knowledge builds confidence, confidence builds enthusiasm, and enthusiasm SELLS." He was teaching us how important it was to learn everything we could about the cars we were selling, the cars we were selling against, as well as learn everything we could about the people we were selling to. That was knowledge that would give us confidence, which would make us enthusiastic about our interactions with our customers. And that enthusiasm is what made the sale.

A phrase that pays:

> "Knowledge builds confidence, confidence builds enthusiasm, and enthusiasm sells."

I am a naturally enthusiastic person, so what I worked on was learning how to share that enthusiasm with customers. While in that job, I figured out a way to do that in a manner that leveraged my sense of humor as well as my sense of drama.

Along a route that we typically used for demo rides, there was an office building that had those reflective mirror windows. I made sure that we would be driving by that building right after I had switched places with the customer and they were behind the wheel. As we began to drive by that building, right next to it, I would suddenly say, “Oh! Stop! Real quick, stop.” They would stop and be a little startled; then I’d say, “Look to your left.”

They would see the reflection of themselves sitting in the driver’s seat of a brand-new car.

Almost all of them would look over at me and say, “You did that on purpose.”

I’d shrug, smile, and say, “Yep. But it’s pretty cool, isn’t it?”

We’d both get to laugh and continue the test drive. But now that customer was in a nice, positive place while driving that car.

Student Takeaways

- "Enthusiasm is contagious."
- Learning about products and people builds confidence, which leads to enthusiasm.
- Create ways to share your enthusiasm.

Reflection Exercise

Think about a time you felt very enthusiastic. What was it that you knew or learned that led to that enthusiasm?

Application Challenge

You're not always going to feel enthusiastic. Try this "trick." Say out loud the phrase, "I feel great," three times in a row, each time with a little more emphasis, the last time almost shouting it. How do you feel after that third effort?

Lanier Sales – Embrace Hard Things

My first sales job was selling dictation equipment for Lanier, and that company was known for being the "Marine Corps of Professional Sales." As salespeople, we were viewed as the best because everyone knew how hard Lanier made things for its people. Yes, there was high turnover, and in the "turn and burn" world of employers, Lanier was the leader. You either learned how to deal with the challenges and excelled, or you flamed out. That was simple.

For starters, everyone was on straight commission. There was a very small draw paid in your first few months, but you only got paid for what you sold—no exceptions. You also had to pay for your own inventory. If you checked out a recorder or some tapes as supplies, that expense went on your paycheck.

We had to be in the office every morning at 7:00 a.m. for a half-hour sales meeting that started the day. You were allowed to get supplies for the day and could talk to other reps, but you had to be out of the office heading to your territory no later than 8:00 a.m. At least once every week, either a senior salesperson or a manager rode with you to evaluate your performance throughout the day. They would also offer advice and reinforce training.

We were required to hold at least two meetings per day with at least one demo. On top of that, we had to make 45 cold calls per day, bringing home those business cards to be counted by our manager. Then we were back in the office by 4:00 p.m. for an afternoon meeting to go over results and prioritize our evening call list to get future appointments. That session began at 4:30, and we had a room set aside for that purpose.

Phones lined the walls with sort of half desks about chest high, mounted to the wall. They were angled with a lip on them so your Daytimer (the old-school, manual Outlook calendar) could sit up there along with a couple of cards, but you couldn't set a drink or something there. You were there for one purpose: to call as many people as you could and schedule as many appointments as you could before people stopped answering their phones that night.

This made work hard, but we got results. At least those of us who learned to embrace the "suck" to maintain focus and intensity.

Student Takeaways

- Get comfortable being uncomfortable.
- "Hard environments can be your competitive advantage."
- Don't avoid pressure; use it to grow.
- "Easy" rarely leads anywhere worth going.

Reflection Exercise

What hard things are you avoiding right now? Why?

How would your life change if you ran toward it for two weeks?

Application Challenge

Pick one hard thing you've been dodging (class, conver-sation, workout). Do it three times this week. Track how you feel before versus after.

7

Curiosity and Growth

"Gorillas in the Cage" – Ask Better Questions

I HAVE LONG HAD a habit of asking a lot of questions, especially the simple question, "Why?" I do this to understand, not because I think something is being done wrong. I began doing that because of a story I once heard: the gorillas in the cage.

The story goes that scientists put five gorillas in a cage in their lab. In the center of the cage was a set of stairs with a bunch of bananas hanging from the ceiling above it. If a gorilla climbed the stairs, it could easily reach the bananas. But when the first gorilla started to climb the stairs toward the bananas, the scientists blasted it with a fire hose, knocking it off the stairs. A while later, another gorilla began to climb the stairs, and the scientists blasted it with the fire hose, too. This time they also blasted all the gorillas even if they weren't near the stairs.

The gorillas didn't go near the bananas again.

So, the scientists removed a gorilla and replaced it with a new one. That gorilla almost immediately went for the bananas, and the scientists hit it with the fire hose along with all the other gorillas. They replaced a couple more gorillas. This time, as one of the new gorillas started for the stairs, the others attacked it and knocked it away from the stairs. The scientists noticed that the meanest, most vicious gorillas during the attack were the ones that had never been hit with the fire hose. They'd never even seen it. Finally, the scientists had replaced all the gorillas with ones that had never been hit with the fire hose.

And none of them ever went near the bananas. Why?

Because that's the way we've always done it.

So, "why" became a question I asked a lot. I discovered that many, many times, a process was in place to deal with something that was no longer an issue. There was no reason to keep it in place. By recognizing that fact, organizations were able to move forward past something they had no idea was holding them back.

Again and again, we found processes with no purpose. Removing them sped everything up.

Student Takeaways

- Systems often outlive their purpose.
- Ask "Why?" when you hear, "That's how we've always done it."
- Great ideas die where questions aren't welcome.
- Progress begins with curiosity.

Reflection Exercise

Name one rule or procedure at school or work that seems pointless. Why does it exist?

If you could change it, what would improve?

Application Challenge

For one week, ask "Why?" in one situation per day. Take notes on what you learn and what you can simplify.

8

It Takes Energy and Effort

Tryouts - Show some hustle.

WHEN WE WERE KIDS, you had to try out to get on the little league teams. On a weekend, every kid who had signed up for baseball, for example, would come out to the fields and go through a series of workouts while all the coaches watched and took notes. The purpose was really to create a way to balance the teams because the coaches would then meet later in the week and rotate through a draft of sorts, picking their teams.

All of us saw it as a competition and an opportunity to see how we compared to each other in throwing, fielding, and hitting.

I was not a fast runner and did not have a great glove; however, I could put the bat on the ball pretty well. So, my dad would give me the same advice right before I'd go out for a fielding or throwing workout.

"Show some hustle."

I took that to heart and honestly went a little overboard at times. For instance, sometimes when I'd hit what should be a single, I'd turn and run hard toward second base. We were kids, and I knew there stood a good chance that someone would make a bad throw or just miss the catch, especially if they were caught off guard. So, it worked more often than it should have. I'd get a double just because I pushed hard.

In the field, I'd move toward a ball hit at me as opposed to waiting for it to come. Here, I'd be the one mishandling a catch, but the coaches liked the fact that I attacked it instead of just sitting back. Basically, I would constantly be bouncing, moving, and ready for the next test.

I never sat still or looked disengaged.

By being more energetic and taking a more aggressive approach to the task, I stood out. I even got better over time because of that effort.

I couldn't always make a great play, but I could always put in more effort than the others around me. That was one thing I knew I could control. And that's what got me noticed in a positive light by the people evaluating my performance.

Student Takeaways

- "Effort" is a controllable advantage.
- "Hustle" and "energy" get positive attention.
- Pushing yourself accelerates both learning and skill development.
- People remember those who work hard more than they remember those who are perfect.

Reflection Exercise

Identify one area today (school, work, sports, relationships) where you know you are not the most skilled—but where "hustle" could help you catch up or surpass others.

What would "showing some hustle" look like there?

How would your life change if you ran toward it for two weeks?

Application Challenge

For the next seven days, choose one daily activity (studying, practice, work, exercise, chores—anything) and decide how you will show extra hustle.

- Start earlier.
- Go harder.
- Solve one more problem.
- Read for 10 more minutes.

- Ask one more question.
- "Try again rather than stop."

Track your effort each day — nothing complicated — just note:

- What you did.
- How much extra effort you put in.
- What changed?

At the end of the week, reflect:

- Did someone notice?
- Did you get better at something?
- Did opportunities open that wouldn't have otherwise?

The goal isn't perfection; it's proving to yourself that effort compounds.

Getting the Job - Going the Extra Mile

Ron had been working in the accounting department of Oracle as a Tax Manager, and he kept seeing how much money the salespeople were making—way more than he was. Now, Ron is a competitive person. He wrestled at the collegiate level, got a degree in accounting, and also went to law school. He was smart.

Ron knew so much about the software Oracle was selling and was intimately aware of the benefits it provided its users—probably more so than the salespeople out there selling it. So, he wanted to reach out to the Director of Sales about getting hired.

But Ron also knew that it was unlikely this guy would see him as anything other than an accountant. After all, Ron didn't have any experience selling; he just knew where he wanted to go.

So, instead of picking up the phone and calling him, Ron got in his car and drove to North Carolina, where the director lived.

He presented his argument like a lawyer would a court case and got hired.

His career went "ballistic" after that.

Student Takeaways

- Sometimes, an obstacle is how someone perceives you; effort can change that.
- Going beyond ordinary shows seriousness and conviction.
- Initiative can outweigh inexperience.
- People hire courage and preparation, not just résumés.

Reflection Exercise

Think of a goal you have right now (job, internship, project, team position).

What's the standard way people pursue it?

What would be a bolder, more memorable approach?

Application Challenge

Pick one opportunity you want: a job, internship, audition, mentor conversation, or leadership role. This week, do one thing 99% of other people won't do, such as:

- *Show up in person.*
- *Record a personalized video pitch.*
- *Build a mini deck showing your plan for the role.*
- *Research the team and send tailored recommendations.*
- *Ask to "shadow" someone for a day.*
- *Complete a relevant project before being asked.*

Document:

- *What you did*
- *How the other person responded.*
- *What you learned*

Even if the answer is "not now," you will:

- *Stand out*
- *Build confidence.*
- *Learn faster.*
- *Strengthen your reputation.*

The win is taking the extraordinary step — that's where the breakthroughs happen.

PART IV

Consistency (C)

9

Consistency Creates Excellence

"Cancer Recovery – One Year to Marathon"

ON NOVEMBER 8, 2008, I was diagnosed with throat cancer. I went through surgeries and months of radiation treatment. Towards the end of my treatments, I caught a nasty bug, which was very bad since my immune system was at its lowest point.

I lost 20 pounds in two and a half days.

I was so weak I couldn't get to the top of a flight of stairs without having to rest and catch my breath. Because of that, I swore to myself I would never be that weak again.

As part of my recovery, I began walking every day, which turned into running. I kept running longer distances, faster, and gained my strength back. On November 8, 2009, I ran the Outer Banks Marathon. I went from calling my kids to tell them I had cancer to running a marathon in exactly one year.

I had never been able to run that far before. I also discovered that I was pretty fast—almost as fast as I had been back in high school over 25 years earlier. A friend of mine told me about Masters Track and gave me some guidance on how to train. While I had started to place fairly high in local 5Ks, I wasn't doing all that great on the track. However, I was approaching training far differently than I had when I was in high school. Back then, I wouldn't push hard during hill or track repeats because they were so damn uncomfortable. If I hurt or got out of breath, I'd just slow down.

But now, whenever those feelings cropped up, I reminded myself of what it was like to collapse just trying to climb a flight of stairs, and that this discomfort was nothing compared to the pain of head and neck radiation. I fell in love with feeling strong and would get fired up every time I stepped onto or near a track. So, I kept pushing. I kept working out almost every single day. And I got faster.

I also didn't skip days just because of the weather. I wasn't going to let the weather be an excuse on race day, so I wouldn't let it be an excuse during training.

I became more consistent.

I started improving and even won some races here and there. I kept pushing myself and fell into a nice rhythm of training and racing. Then one day, a friend pointed out to me a website that showed where I was ranked in my events. I found out that I was ranked in the top 25 in the U.S. in the 800m run and number 73 in the world. I couldn't believe it, so I just kept going.

Over the years, I have been ranked in the top 20 in the U.S. at least five times in different events, including achieving one All-American standard. I've podiumed over 30 times in state, national, and even international meets—all because I pushed hard and did it consistently.

That's the heart of this book: "Consistency turns effort into excellence."

Student Takeaways

- "Consistency is the force multiplier of talent."
- Use past hardships as fuel for present discipline.
- "Show up when it's boring; that's where progress hides."
- "Excellence is a pattern, not a moment."

Reflection Exercise

What small daily habit would most improve your life in 90 days?

What obstacle typically breaks your streak? How will you handle it next time?

Application Challenge

Pick one habit tied to your goals (study hour, workout, outreach, practice). Do it every day for 30 days. Track it. Miss a day? Start a new streak immediately.

PART V

Putting It All Together

I set out to create what I believed to be the formula for success: an actual mathematical equation that considered the variables, constants, and any other inputs that impacted the results. As I talked with my friends and researched through my memory and old sales books, I identified as many of those inputs as I could find. Then I started building out the equation, beginning with the result I wanted to achieve: excellence.

What I found was that preparation was critical but didn't have to be something drawn from a book or seminar. It didn't have to be boring. It could be achieved simply by living our lives with intent—living with a purpose in mind, beginning with what we wanted the most out of life. These things would most likely be things we enjoyed or were passionate about, which meant that preparing could be very easy at times. I also learned that sometimes it wouldn't be, but by keeping my eye on where I wanted to go, I could more easily see what preparations had to be made in order for me to get there.

Then I saw how being prepared positively impacted an opportunity when it showed up. We all get opportunities just about every day, but unless we're prepared to take advantage of them, they just fall to the side. It's like seeing an ad for a huge, high-definition TV for only a couple of hundred dollars. That's a great opportunity to get a great TV, but if you don't have access to those couple of hundred dollars, you miss out.

I learned that those moments when preparation meets opportunity aren't as rare as I originally thought. However, when those moments exploded for folks, I found there were other factors in play. This is where how people reacted to those moments made a huge difference. As I dug into that, I found that when people applied enthusiasm, energy, and effort to a moment when preparation met an opportunity, the results improved exponentially.

Finally, it was clear that this wasn't a one-and-done situation. Yes, Dwayne made the choice and took the job with Ray Charles. But then he had to deliver. Ron got hired as a salesperson, but then he had to sell something. Those moments are just that: moments. They're there, and then they're gone. So, we need to keep preparing, keep applying enthusiasm, energy, and effort to everything we do.

We need to be consistent.

$$\mathbf{E=[(P+O)e^3]C}$$

Where:

E = Excellence
P = Preparation
O = Opportunity
e^3 = Enthusiasm, Energy and Effort
C = Consistency

I've been thinking about how to give this a super, pump-you-up finish, but everything I've thought of comes across as silly. You've got the formula and done some exercises that will help you apply this to your day-to-day life. It's just up to you now to do something about it. You need to commit to it.

Did you know you can see the definition of "commitment" in a plate of ham and eggs?

The chicken was involved, but the pig was committed.

Once you decide on a goal and identify the steps you need to take to achieve it, it's up to you to make sure those steps get done. No one else is going to do it for you.

Be the pig. Be committed.

My suggestion is that you think about this formula each morning, consider how you want to be remembered, and envision where you'd like to see yourself someday.

Then find ways to prepare yourself for an opportunity to achieve those goals.

Taking that long view is definitely going to make it look like something so far away that you'll never get to it. But you will.

A phrase that pays:

> How do you eat an elephant?
> One bite at a time.

Get eating.

www.ingramcontent.com/pod-product-compliance
Lightning Source LLC
LaVergne TN
LVHW051136210926
848482LV00006B/327